· no A.R.

D1568194

LEADERS OF THE
MIDDLE AGES™

ELEANOR OF AQUITAINE

The Richest Queen in Medieval Europe

LEADERS OF THE MIDDLE AGES™

ELEANOR OF AQUITAINE

The Richest Queen in Medieval Europe

David Hilliam

The Rosen Publishing Group, Inc., New York

Published in 2005 by the Rosen Publishing Group, Inc.
29 East 21st Street, New York, NY 10010

First Edition

Library of Congress Cataloging-in-Publication Data

Hilliam, David.
Eleanor of Aquitaine: the richest queen in medieval
Europe/David Hilliam.—1st ed.
    p. cm.—(Leaders of the Middle Ages)
Includes bibliographical references and index.
ISBN 1-4042-0162-9 (library binding)
1. Eleanor, of Aquitaine, Queen, consort of Henry II, King of
England, 1122?–1204—Juvenile literature. 2. Great Britain—
History—Henry II, 1154–1189—Biography—Juvenile literature.
3. France—History—Louis VII, 1137–1180—Biography—Juvenile
literature. 4. Queens—Great Britain—Biography—Juvenile
literature. 5. Queens—France—Biography—Juvenile literature.
I. Title. II. Series.
DA209.E6H55 2005
942.03'1'092—dc22
                                                    2004000038
Manufactured in the United States of America

On the cover: Inset: Stone tomb effigy of Eleanor of Aquitaine
in the abbey church of Notre Dame de Fontevrault in France.
Background: A page from *Roman de la Rose*, a fifteenth-century
French manuscript.

CONTENTS

Introduction: A Great Medieval Queen 7

CHAPTER 1   Eleanor's Early Life 11

CHAPTER 2   King Louis VII and Queen Eleanor 20

CHAPTER 3   Eleanor, Raymond, Louis, and Henry 32

CHAPTER 4   Queen of England 42

CHAPTER 5   Family Problems 54

CHAPTER 6   Rebellion, Imprisonment, and the Death of Henry 66

CHAPTER 7   Eleanor Rules England for Richard the Lionheart 77

CHAPTER 8   Eleanor's Exciting Final Years 91

Timeline 99

Glossary 100

For More Information 104

For Further Reading 105

Bibliography 106

Index 107

INTRODUCTION: A GREAT MEDIEVAL QUEEN

Eleanor of Aquitaine, the daughter of the Duke of Aquitaine, was sensationally beautiful and outstandingly rich. While her whole life was filled with excitement and danger, her main contribution to history occurred in her later years.

At that time, even though she was quite old, she energetically helped her son, King Richard I of England. She acted as his deputy when he was away from England fighting a Crusade in the Holy Land. Because she had acquired so much political experience and wisdom, Eleanor ruled the country with immense skill and power. Certainly no queen in history has had such a long, varied, or remarkably eventful life.

In 1122, when Eleanor was born, France was divided into about twenty semi-independent regions. Each was governed by its own duke or count. These dukes owed allegiance to the king of France. However, because communication and transportation were slow during medieval times, the regions were isolated. This meant that the dukes could act as leaders in their own territory. Since it would take a long time to receive a response or demand from the king, the dukes were able to run lands as they saw fit. They were so powerful, they would often make the decision of whether or not one of their subjects should live or die. They also had their own armies.

One of the largest and richest of these dukedoms was the southern province of Aquitaine. This is where Eleanor's father, William, was duke. His rule extended into the wealthy neighboring provinces of Poitou and Gascony. The climate of this area of southern France was warm and comfortable. Aquitaine also possessed prosperous farms and vineyards that grew beside the many beautiful rivers of the region. The name "Aquitaine" comes from Latin, meaning "land of waters."

In Eleanor's time, poetry and the arts were much more sophisticated in Aquitaine and the south of France than in the more barbaric north of Europe. Aquitaine was a land of troubadours (poets and

This is a partial view of the tomb effigy (representation) of Eleanor of Aquitaine. The tomb is in the abbey church of Notre Dame de Fontevrault in France. This funerary statue is the only existing artifact that is similar to a portrait of Eleanor. The tomb is made from multicolored stone, and it dates from the thirteenth century. Eleanor is shown with an open book, probably to demonstrate her piety or her intense interest in learning.

musicians). Its lords and ladies wore elaborate and colorful clothes.

When Eleanor came to live in Paris as queen of France (and later in London as queen of England) she brought with her a standard of style and taste which had never been known in either of these capital cities. As a young woman, Eleanor's beauty was legendary. Many poems were written about her. As she grew older, she became increasingly respected and admired for her political abilities. She was a tough ruler, as capable as any man.

Because she was so actively linked to all the important events in twelfth-century France and England, her biography provides valuable insight into the times in which she lived.

ELEANOR'S EARLY LIFE

In 1127, when Eleanor was only five years old, her grandfather, Duke William IX of Aquitaine, died. Her twenty-seven-year-old father succeeded him as Duke William X. At this time, Aquitaine was the largest and richest province in France. Its rulers, the dukes, were more powerful than even the king of France himself. The dukes also owned two other important provinces, Poitou to the west and Gascony to the south. Eleanor had a sister, Petronilla, who was three years younger than herself. She also had a brother, William Aigret, who was about four years younger.

It was expected that as a male, young William Aigret would one day become the next Duke of Aquitaine. Unfortunately, however, a triple tragedy struck the family in 1130. First, Eleanor's father, Duke William, was publicly warned of God's displeasure of him by the saintly preacher Bernard of Clairvaux. This was because he had dared to support a rival pope (Duke William was known for his quick temper and quarrelsome nature). At that time, there was a serious division within the church. The pope, Innocent II, was being opposed by an "anti-pope" named Anacletus. Eleanor's father was supporting Anacletus and Pope Innocent was so offended by Duke William that he excommunicated him. This meant that William was banned from the church, and was considered to be in danger of going to hell when he died. In spite of this, William continued to support Anacletus.

A crisis point came when Duke William burst into a church where Bernard of Clairvaux was preaching against him. Fully armed, William intended to throw Bernard out of the building. However, Bernard showed no fear. He advanced toward William, holding the sacred bread and wine of the Catholic Mass in front of him. This dramatic gesture had a terrifying effect. Suffering from a fit, William collapsed to the ground. He was foaming at the mouth, and for a while he couldn't even move. The episode was regarded as a miraculous warning that showed God's anger against the duke. When he recovered, Duke William, who was extremely upset, admitted that he had been in the wrong.

This image from a French illuminated manuscript shows a knight dressed in pilgrim's clothes with a long staff, a pilgrim's hat, and a small bag. What's interesting here is that this pilgrim seems to have abandoned his armor (to his left). This indicates that he has chosen to leave his previous life as a knight. It seems that instead, he preferred to embark on a possibly dangerous pilgrimage similar to the one Eleanor's father would undertake. This image, a page from *Le Pélerinage de Vie Humaine* (The Pilgrimage of Human Life), is by Guillaume de Deguilleville and dates from 1393.

Two other family disasters followed. Quite unexpectedly, both Eleanor's mother and her brother, William Aigret, became ill and died. This, of course, left Eleanor, age eight, as the heiress to her father's extensive lands. His lands consisted of a quarter of present-day France. Eleanor must have been increasingly aware of just how important she had become—arguably, the most important girl in Europe.

Her father felt that it was necessary for him to marry again, as he hoped to have another son. But before looking for a wife, he decided to make a pilgrimage to the shrine of St. James of Compostela in Spain. He hoped to seek forgiveness for his sins and to pray for a male heir. Such a pilgrimage was commonly thought to be a way of pleasing God. It would be a long and dangerous journey. He also realized that his absence from Aquitaine raised the issue of who should succeed him if he failed to return.

Accordingly, in 1136, on Eleanor's fourteenth birthday, William assembled all his vassals (noblemen who owed him allegiance) to his palace. He commanded them to swear homage to Eleanor and acknowledge her as the heiress of Aquitaine, Poitou, and Gascony. By doing this, William felt he could go on the pilgrimage with reasonable certainty that Eleanor would be respected and obeyed in his absence.

ELEANOR AS A TEENAGER

Eleanor was very mature and forceful even at fourteen. She is reported to have been tall and strikingly beautiful. Her intelligence, wit, and lively manner attracted the attention of many men. She loved fine

THE CEREMONY OF HOMAGE

The ceremony of homage was common in the Middle Ages, when allegiance, or "fealty" as it was sometimes called, was openly expressed to ensure that obedience and loyalty could be counted on. The vassal (the person who was expressing his loyalty) would kneel down and put his hands between those of his master or mistress and swear to be obedient. In return, the master or mistress would promise to give the vassal protection from his enemies.

clothes, and because of her wealth, she had the opportunity to dress in the most expensive fashions. She often wore silk dresses and gowns embroidered with gold thread. Above all, she loved jewelry. All her life, she collected fascinating and valuable items to wear with her wonderful dresses.

But Eleanor was not just a spoiled teenager who loved finery. At that time, girls rarely learned to read or write. However, Eleanor was given a good education in literature, foreign languages (including Latin), and music. She also learned the

This equestrian portrait (so called because it features a figure on a horse), showing a well-dressed troubadour, illustrates the type of fine clothing and fabric that Eleanor liked to wear. A troubadour was a poet who composed works of chivalry and courtly love, an important literary subject that started in eleventh-century France. Troubadors were minstrels who traveled from castle to castle to entertain lords and ladies. The portrait is from a thirteenth-century French book illustration.

traditional skills of needlework and household management. In addition, she was an excellent sportswoman. She had learned to ride horses when she was quite young, and she also liked hunting and falconry. She was an attractive, energetic, and clever young woman. She would make a fine wife for any future husband.

DUKE WILLIAM PLANS HER MARRIAGE

As her father made preparations to go on his pilgrimage to Compostela, he became increasingly worried that some of his vassals might be interested in marrying Eleanor. He felt that she was far too valuable a person to marry a man of inferior status. Duke William was determined to do the best for his daughter. Accordingly, he put her under the protection of the king of France, Louis VI. William knew that King Louis would protect Eleanor against any possible enemies. He also hoped that the king would see Eleanor as a possible bride for his son, Prince Louis. If so, Eleanor would be the future queen of France.

Dressed in the rough clothes of a humble pilgrim, Duke William and a few companions left for Compostela in February 1137. They arrived there in April. Unfortunately, along the way, William drank contaminated water and became extremely ill. He realized that he was dying and urgently needed to make his final will. He begged his companions to go to King Louis immediately and ask him to arrange for his son to marry Eleanor. However, he ordered that Eleanor's huge land possessions should not be incorporated into the king's. Instead, he wanted them to remain in Eleanor's possession. When he had made his will,

This lovely fourteenth-century illustration from a French illuminated manuscript page shows the magnificent and lavish wedding of Eleanor of Aquitaine and King Louis VII. The manuscript is called *Les Grandes Chroniques de France*, (The Great Chronicles of France). Eleanor is elegantly and stylishly dressed in a fur-trimmed cape. As was her style and preference, her wedding attire was made of the most luxurious fabrics that were available at the time.

William was carried into the cathedral at Compostela, where he died shortly after. He was buried there before the high altar.

As a result of his death, Eleanor, who was now fifteen, became Duchess of Aquitaine and Gascony, and Countess of Poitou. This was a huge responsibility. Very few leaders had acquired vast possessions at such an early age. Furthermore, for a girl to do so was unheard of.

King Louis VI of France was almost speechless with delight when he heard the news that Duke William of Aquitaine had asked for Eleanor to marry his son. The king, (who was nicknamed "Louis the Fat" because of his obesity) knew that if the couple had children, the rest of France would be united with Aquitaine, Gascony, and Poitou forever. Prince Louis was just a year or so older than Eleanor—it seemed to be a perfect match.

Eleanor's bridegroom-to-be, sixteen-year-old Prince Louis, was obedient and dutiful. If his father required him to marry the Duchess of Aquitaine, then he would do so without question. Accordingly, on July 25, 1137, Eleanor and Louis were given a magnificent wedding in Bordeaux Cathedral. Afterward, they set off for Paris to begin their new life together. However, less than a week later, a messenger brought the newlywed teenage couple the startling news that King Louis the Fat had just died. Louis and Eleanor were now king and queen of France!

KING LOUIS VII AND QUEEN ELEANOR

CHAPTER 2

Eleanor soon found that her new lifestyle was far less appealing than what she was used to in sunny Aquitaine. Paris in those days was quite unlike the beautiful and exciting city it is today. The buildings were small and drab. The palace where she would live was a dark, crumbling tower with little light and ventilation. There was no tradition of courtly entertainment such as she was accustomed to.

Eleanor immediately began to introduce more civilized customs and manners. For example, she encouraged singers, poets, and musicians to visit her. She fired the choirmaster in the royal palace and replaced him with someone far more talented. She was forceful in demanding high standards in what had until then been a somewhat simple and even barbaric court.

However, a deeper cause for Eleanor's dissatisfaction was the character of her new husband. Eleanor had been given no part in choosing her husband, and she soon realized that she and Louis had totally different personalities and interests.

Louis was a shy, unworldly boy who had been a "child monk"—a boy who had been learning the disciplined lifestyle of a monastery. In fact, Louis had been destined to enter the church until his elder brother was killed in a riding accident.

Louis's whole life was centered on religion. Even when it was apparent that he would be king, he continued his devout studies under Suger,

During the time when Eleanor was in Paris, the city was dark and gloomy. This is an image of the famous Notre Dame Cathedral on Ile de la Cité in Paris. Its gothic style of architecture suggests how drab it would be to walk in a city of gray sky and gray stones. The construction of Notre Dame Cathedral began in 1163.

the all-important abbot of Saint-Denis, near Paris. Even after his marriage, Louis was still leading this church-centered life. He would join the cathedral choir at Notre Dame, fast with the monks, and assist at mass. He dressed like a humble priest and took no interest at all in the pomp and ceremony of royalty. Louis's attitude toward life could hardly have been more different from that of Eleanor. She was used to the permissive society of Aquitaine, where her own grandfather had lived for years with his mistress.

Needless to say, Louis was still too young to make wise decisions for himself. He relied heavily on Abbot Suger to tell him what to do. Suger had been his father's chief adviser. Because of this, it was only natural for Louis to continue to rely on the abbot's experience in ruling the country.

Meanwhile, Abbot Suger was determined to exclude Eleanor from having any say in governing the country. He distrusted her, disliking her obvious love of luxury. Other churchmen also criticized her. In fact, even the most influential priest of the time, Bernard of Clairvaux, was shocked by Eleanor's extravagantly ornate dresses. He thought they were sinful. Nevertheless, Eleanor brushed aside any criticisms and was determined to take part in making decisions in ruling France. Though Louis disliked violence,

Eleanor urged him to wage war against nobles who were rebelling against him.

In 1143, when he was fighting the armies of Count Theobald of Champagne, Louis was inadvertently responsible for a terrible disaster. More than a thousand people were burned to death in the cathedral of Vitry. The people of the town had sought shelter in the building as Louis's army set fire to the town. Unfortunately, the fire spread to the cathedral. Louis saw what was happening. He could hear the people's screams and smell their burning flesh. He was horrified by what he had done.

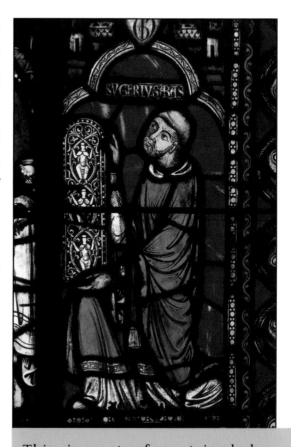

This is part of a stained-glass window in the ambulatory of Saint-Denis Cathedral in France. The stained glass features a depiction of Abbot Suger, who founded Saint-Denis in 1137. He was responsible for decorating it. He commissioned the best painters he could find. They came from many different regions and reworked the crumbling walls with gold, silver, precious gems, and wonderful textiles.

Louis returned to Paris quite devastated. Because of his guilt, he could hardly sleep for weeks afterward. Eventually, he decided that the only way to make amends for his great sin was to make a pilgrimage to Jerusalem.

THE POPE CALLS FOR A SECOND CRUSADE IN THE HOLY LAND

However, events in the Holy Land were to demand more of Louis than a mere pilgrimage. In December 1144, the Christian-held county of Edessa was recaptured by the Muslim Turks. Edessa was one of the crusader states established after the First Crusade. The First Crusade, which took place from 1096 to 1099, had been successful for the Christian crusaders, as they had captured Jerusalem. However, with the fall of Edessa, it seemed that all their efforts were being undone. The pope was desperately worried and called for another Crusade. Who would now save the Holy Land?

Although, at that time, Louis was probably the least military-minded monarch in the world, the thought of a crusade greatly appealed to him. Louis felt that by taking part in a crusade, he would please God and his sins would be forgiven. Without

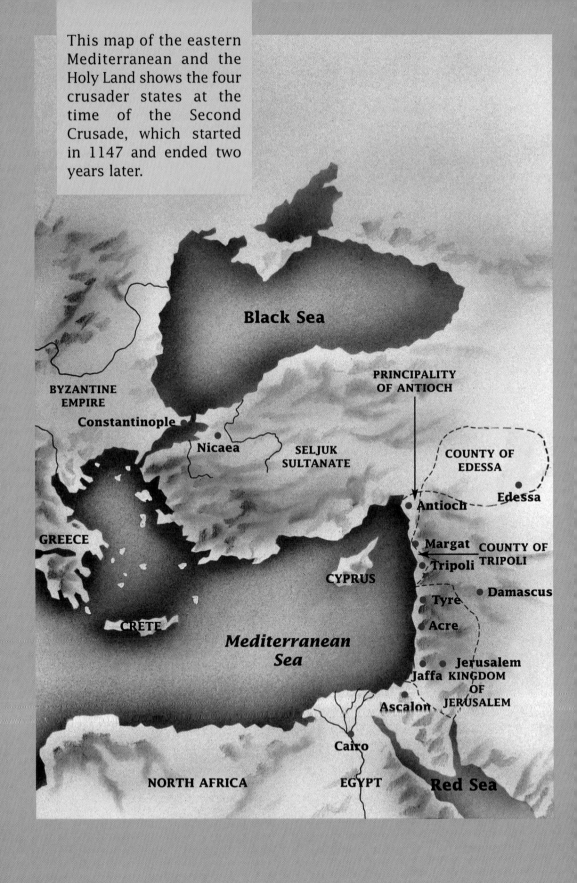

This map of the eastern Mediterranean and the Holy Land shows the four crusader states at the time of the Second Crusade, which started in 1147 and ended two years later.

Black Sea

PRINCIPALITY OF ANTIOCH

BYZANTINE EMPIRE

Constantinople

Nicaea

SELJUK SULTANATE

COUNTY OF EDESSA

Antioch

Edessa

GREECE

Margat

COUNTY OF TRIPOLI

Tripoli

CYPRUS

Damascus

Tyre

CRETE

Acre

Mediterranean Sea

Jaffa

Jerusalem

KINGDOM OF JERUSALEM

Ascalon

Cairo

NORTH AFRICA

EGYPT

Red Sea

THE CRUSADER STATES

The First Crusade (1096–1099) had been successful for the Christians, as they managed to conquer and occupy Jerusalem. Afterward, many crusaders (mostly French) stayed in the Holy Land while occupying four states, which were known as *Outremer*, French for "overseas." Each state—the Principality of Antioch, the county of Edessa, the county of Tripoli, and the kingdom of Jerusalem—was independent and was ruled by its own king or prince. The French had developed a small empire in the Holy Land, and Eleanor's uncle Raymond was one of its leaders.

even consulting his advisers, Louis announced that he would wage a Second Crusade to rescue Edessa from the Muslim Turks. Abbot Suger was alarmed. What would happen during the king's absence? And more important, what would happen if the king were killed? Eleanor had just given birth to a baby girl, but France desperately needed a male heir before Louis put himself at risk by leading a crusade.

Abbot Suger was even more alarmed when he heard that Eleanor had declared her intention of accompanying the king and forming her own

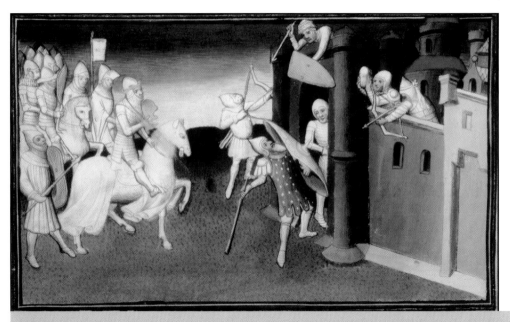

This is a fifteenth-century French illuminated manuscript page that illustrates a scene from the First Crusade (1096–1099). Eight principal crusades took place between 1096 and 1270. This scene shows the conquest of the state of Jerusalem in the Third Crusade (1189–1191) by the Saracens-Muslim warriors. This particular battle was led by Sultan Saladin on October 3, 1187. Eleanor and King Louis of France took part in the Second Crusade (1147–1149). Eleanor's uncle Raymond was also involved in the Second Crusade.

contingent of female crusaders! Could anything be more foolish? Suger advised them both to stay in France. However, Louis and Eleanor refused to listen to any words of caution. For Eleanor, it was an exciting adventure, and for Louis, it was a way of saving his soul.

Eleanor persuaded a number of noble ladies to accompany her. Hundreds of other less aristocratic women also volunteered, offering to help nurse the wounded. While Louis gathered his army together, Eleanor toured her own provinces, stirring up enthusiasm for the great enterprise. The plan was that the French army would meet up with the German army. The French army consisted of about 100,000 soldiers. Most of these were Eleanor's own vassals from Aquitaine. Meanwhile, the German army, which was led by Emperor Conrad, numbered about 10,000. The armies would proceed to the Holy Land via Constantinople, the capital of what was then known as the Byzantine Empire. Constantinople is now present-day Istanbul in Turkey.

Eleanor was in very good spirits. She is reported to have dressed herself up as Penthesilea, the legendary leader of the Amazons. The Amazons were a race of female warriors in Greek mythology. A contemporary historian, Gervase of Canterbury, described the costume of Eleanor and her ladies as white tunics decorated with red crosses, large feathered hats, and white knee-length "buskins," or boots. She took along an enormous amount of baggage, too. This included clothes, furs, tents, jewelry, beds, washbasins, and every other luxury that could be thought of. She took no notice of those—including Louis—who criticized her for packing so many unnecessary items. In May 1147, the French army set off.

DISASTERS FOR THE CRUSADERS

The German army was the first to arrive at Constantinople, and then it headed south. It had just left the city when it was ambushed by the Turks and suffered a terrible defeat. More than nine-tenths of the army was slaughtered. Emperor Conrad, who was wounded, only just managed to escape. When Louis and Eleanor caught up with Conrad and the remaining German army, they were devastated to discover what had happened. Conrad was so ill that he had to return to Constantinople. Meanwhile, Louis and Eleanor struggled ahead through mountainous countryside in terrible winter conditions. At the same time, the Turks, who were watching them, were waiting for an opportunity to strike.

As they came to a particularly difficult mountain path, Louis ordered one of his commanders to continue on with Eleanor and her ladies and a small advance party. The commander, Geoffrey de Rançon, helped them set up camp on a plateau before the next mountain pass. Louis would then follow with the main army and Eleanor's baggage. However, when de Rançon, Eleanor, and her ladies got to the appointed place, they decided it was too windswept and uncomfortable. They journeyed onward through the pass,

Though Eleanor's intentions were good, the Crusades were really no place for ladies of the time. These exceedingly violent and bloody battles were tough enough for trained warriors and soldiers, as is illustrated in this illuminated manuscript image of a fight against the Moors in the state of Jerusalem. The manuscript dates from the fourteenth century.

until they came to a pleasant valley. It was a fatal mistake. The Turks knew that the main army would eventually follow Eleanor and her fellow travelers. The Turks had only to wait for their enemies to arrive.

When Louis and his troops got to the place where they had arranged to meet the advance party, they found it deserted. Puzzled, they decided they would go on through the pass. Savagely, the Turks swooped on the unsuspecting

French army and slashed it to pieces. Louis's horse was killed underneath him and he had to scramble for safety. The Turks killed 7,000 crusaders. They also captured much of their equipment and sup- plies—including the enormous extra baggage belonging to Eleanor and her ladies.

When Louis and what little remained of his army finally met up with Eleanor and her companions, he was furious with Geoffrey de Rançon for disobeying his orders. By then, Louis's men were in a sorry state. They had lost most of their belongings, and many were dying of sickness and starvation. Louis was in no mood to march overland. Accordingly, he decided to ship as much of his army as he could to his first destination—the city of Antioch.

Antioch was a beautiful, prosperous, and ancient city. It was also under threat by the Muslim Turks who had captured the neighboring Christian state of Edessa. Louis and his military commanders looked forward to a warm welcome when they arrived. As for Eleanor, she must have been delighted at the prospect. Its ruler, the prince of Antioch, was her uncle, Raymond of Poitiers.

ELEANOR, RAYMOND, LOUIS, AND HENRY

CHAPTER 3

1
2
4
5
6
7
8

Because Raymond feared being attacked by the Turks, he was delighted to welcome Louis and his army. He hoped that together they could recapture Edessa and make the whole area safe for the occupying Christians. This, after all, was what the Crusades intended to do.

Raymond gave Louis and Eleanor an extravagant welcome. He presented them with jewels, lucky charms, and precious relics. He held banquets in their honor and allowed them to stay in his own luxurious palace. Eleanor was thrilled to receive silk gowns from her uncle.

Raymond, her father's younger brother, was tall, handsome, and incredibly strong. He possessed all the knightly skills of horsemanship and handling weapons of war. About thirty-six, he was only ten years older than Eleanor, and there were many things they had in common. It soon became obvious to all that Raymond and Eleanor were spending a great deal of time in one another's company. Rumors began to spread, suggesting that their relationship was more romantic than that of uncle and niece.

Louis was well aware of these rumors and tension built up between Raymond, Eleanor, and himself. This was not helped by the fact that Louis planned to travel southward to Jerusalem instead of going along with Raymond's plans to march northward to recapture Edessa. Raymond was furious that he was being ignored, and Eleanor openly took his side. She told Louis that if he went to Jerusalem without first attacking Edessa, she would stay behind in Antioch with Raymond. The rift between Eleanor and Louis grew more serious when she announced that she wanted a divorce.

The reason Eleanor gave for wanting a divorce was that she had discovered that she and Louis were related to one another as distant cousins. It was the usual loophole—when royal couples wanted to separate, they would "discover" that they were distantly related. It was increasingly obvious that Eleanor had been brooding over the possibility of divorce from Louis for some time. Now she had made her wishes clear.

Louis was devastated. He was no longer welcome in Antioch and his wife despised him. His reaction was swift. He ordered his army to secretly prepare to leave the city. Without warning, Eleanor was woken up at midnight and forced to accompany her husband to Jerusalem. She didn't get a chance to say good-bye to Raymond. A contemporary historian, William of Tyre (circa 1130–1185), in his book, *A History of Deeds Done Beyond the Sea,* bluntly remarked that Louis's departure was "shameful."

LOUIS IS PARDONED FOR HIS SINS

About six weeks later, in May 1148, Louis arrived in Jerusalem, where he was warmly welcomed. He was delighted to at last visit the Church of the Holy Sepulchre and to receive pardon for all of his sins. Afterward, he and his lords were taken to other holy shrines. However, Eleanor was now in disgrace because of her affair with her uncle. She was not

This map is from the *Chronicles of the Crusades*, written by Robert le Moine de Reims. A French abbot, de Reims was present at the conquest of Jerusalem in 1099.

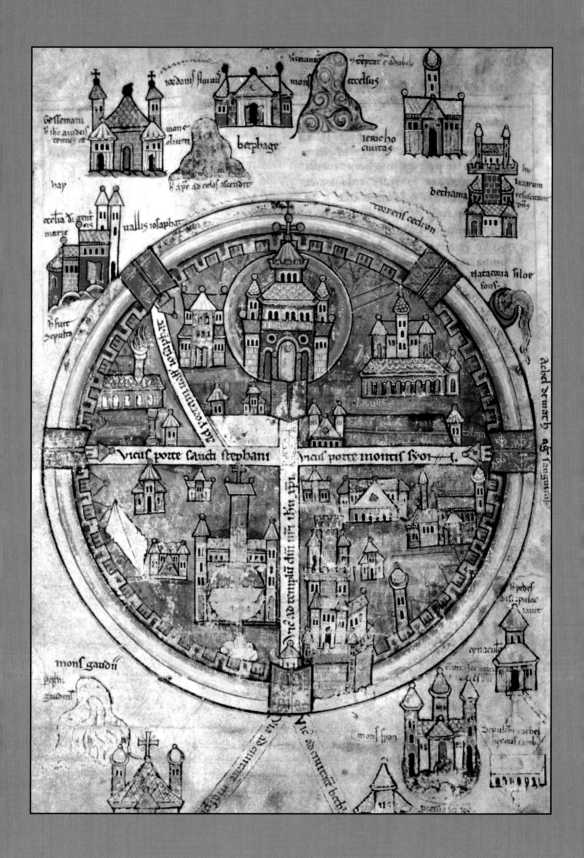

reported to have accompanied Louis to any of these sacred places.

The problem now facing Louis was what he should do next. The local rulers in Jerusalem had no wish to help Louis capture Edessa. In addition, Raymond of Antioch was declaring himself against the whole idea of carrying on with the crusade. Louis had to do something, if only to prove to the Christian world that this Second Crusade had achieved something. Foolishly, he decided to attack Damascus, a Muslim city to the northeast of Jerusalem. Sadly, however, the results were disastrous. His troops were defeated in four days. After this, the whole crusade collapsed. His soldiers deserted him. It was evident that he would have to return home to France and acknowledge his failure.

Eleanor's feelings can only be guessed at as she accompanied the pathetic remnant of the crusade home by sea. English historian William of Newburgh (circa 1135–1200) noted in his book, *The History of English Affairs*, that there were many quarrels between Eleanor and Louis. He wrote that she "was greatly offended with the King's conduct, and complained that she was married to a monk, not a king." The events of the previous months must have made her more determined than ever to demand a divorce.

ADVENTURES ON THE WAY
HOME TO FRANCE

On their journey home, Eleanor and Louis traveled in separate ships to Italy. Unfortunately, Eleanor's ship was blown off course in a violent storm. When Louis arrived in Italy, he didn't know where she was, or even whether she was still alive. What had happened was that Eleanor had landed in Sicily. She had become sick, probably due to exhaustion. As a result, she had to rest for a few weeks. After four months, Eleanor rejoined Louis and together they continued home. They had planned to meet the pope in Rome on the way.

As they set off, Eleanor heard the sickening news that her uncle, Raymond of Antioch, had been killed in a battle with the Muslim leader Nureddin. To prove his victory, Nureddin had cut off Raymond's head and sent it in a silver case to the ruler of Baghdad. It was being exhibited as a trophy of war over the city gate.

Upon their arrival in Rome, Louis and Eleanor were each anxious to raise the question of divorce with the pope. But while Eleanor was desperate for a separation, Louis wanted the marriage to continue. Only the pope, as their spiritual adviser, could make a judgment. He commanded them to stay married. He even told them to sleep together and ordered that a luxurious double bed be prepared for them. Whatever Eleanor may have felt, the result of the pope's effort to bring the couple together was that she became pregnant.

A TROUBLED MARRIAGE

At last, in November 1149, after an absence of nearly two and a half years, the exhausted royal party arrived back in Paris with the remains of the army and ladies' crusade. Louis and Eleanor were welcomed by the citizens, who demonstrated their joy to see their king and queen again. However, no one could hide the fact that their crusade had been a total disaster.

The following year, when Eleanor gave birth to a second girl, even Louis was beginning to think of divorce. He desperately needed sons to succeed the throne. His advisers were telling him to marry again. Only Abbot Suger urged him to stay with Eleanor. He reminded Louis of the huge territory of Aquitaine, which would be the inheritance of their daughter Marie, even if no future son were to be born.

However, for the moment, Louis was more worried about the political situation. His most powerful vassal, Count Geoffrey of Anjou, had conquered the Duchy of Normandy. Geoffrey had given the land to his ambitious teenage son, Henry, and had made him its duke. Henry was only sixteen, but he was already a formidable power. Everyone knew that his aim was to unite Anjou, Normandy, and England to form one great empire. As his mother, Matilda, was a granddaughter of William the Conqueror, he already had a claim to England. She had actually been queen for a few months, but civil war had broken out and she had lost the throne to her cousin Stephen. Because of this, young Henry, Duke of Normandy, was determined to do justice to his mother and bring law and order back to war-torn England.

ELEANOR MEETS HENRY, DUKE OF NORMANDY

Louis was deeply concerned about Henry and his ambitions to form an empire. As Duke of Normandy, Henry was Louis's vassal and therefore obliged to pay him homage. But just how seriously Henry would keep any promise to obey Louis—a promise which he would have to make in his act of homage—was open to question. Henry was young, impetuous, and unpredictable. In the autumn of 1151, Henry arrived in Paris to pay

In March 1152, Eleanor and King Louis VII (also known as Louis the Younger) were divorced. This image, showing their divorce proceedings, is from *Les Grandes Chroniques de France* (The Great Chronicles of France), which was published between 1335 and 1340. Louis VII is pictured in the center, wearing a crown. Those around him are probably clergymen and theologians. They advised that the marriage had not been blessed with a son and heir because Eleanor and he were too closely related—this is called consanguinity.

homage to Louis and to formally receive the dukedom of Normandy from him. It was in Paris that Henry met Eleanor for the first time.

At this time, Henry was eighteen and Eleanor was twenty-nine. However, this age difference didn't prevent them from being attracted to each other. Neither did the fact that Eleanor was still married, and that Henry was Louis's vassal.

Even kings and queens fall in love at first sight, and this is probably what happened. Eleanor was still beautiful, passionate, and yearning for love. For the time being, however, she and Henry kept the matter secret, and no one suspected their plans to marry.

By this time, Louis's advisers agreed that Eleanor's marriage to Louis should be annulled. Even the pope was persuaded to realize that divorce should take place on the grounds of their blood relationship. Accordingly, on March 21, 1152, the foremost bishop of France proclaimed the annulment of their marriage. Louis was given custody of their two young daughters, Marie and Alix. As a result, Eleanor and Louis were now free to remarry, if they chose to do so.

QUEEN OF ENGLAND

Shortly after Henry met Eleanor in Paris, Henry's father, Count Geoffrey of Anjou, died unexpectedly. As a result, Henry inherited the counties of Maine and Anjou. As he already possessed the dukedom of Normandy, it meant that Henry was ruler of three large adjacent parts of France. In theory, however, he held them as a vassal of King Louis.

After her annulment, Eleanor resumed her independent position as Duchess of Aquitaine. A marriage between Henry and Eleanor would unite all these possessions in one vast empire. This empire would stretch from the English Channel to the Pyrenees in the south of France. The formation of such an empire would make Henry and Eleanor the most powerful couple in Europe. Because of this, they made their marriage plans in

Less than two months after Eleanor's divorce from Louis, she and Henry II were married in a quiet ceremony on May 18, 1152, in the Cathedral of Saint-Pierre at Poitiers. Eleanor was thirty and Henry was nineteen. There are no images of this event, but this photo shows the tombs of Eleanor and her husband, King Henry II of England. These sculptures, made of multicolored stone, date from the end of the twelfth century to the beginning of the thirteenth century.

secret. However, they were determined to press ahead with the wedding as soon as possible.

HENRY INVADES ENGLAND

Louis had no idea that this marriage had taken place. When he heard about it, he was furious. It was an insult for a vassal to have "stolen" his former queen. To marry so soon after the annulment was also an act of deliberate rudeness. He felt that Henry should have asked his permission to marry and ordered them both to appear before him. When

THE ENGLISH BARONS AND THE MAGNA CARTA

In medieval England, the word "baron" meant a landowner who held his lands directly from the king. The most important of these were dukes and earls who ruled large tracts, or areas of land, in the name of the king. Some of these barons were so powerful that they were able to defy a king's orders.

In 1215, during the reign of King John, the barons forced the king to sign the famous bill of rights known as the Magna Carta ("the great charter"). This declaration of rights was the first step toward democracy.

The Magna Carta was an important document because it controlled the powers of the king. It was a symbol that the monarch was accountable to others. The creation of this charter meant that the power of the king could be limited by the barons. The document above, the agreement between King John and the barons, indicates that they would all abide by the terms of the Magna Carta. It is dated between June 15 and 25, 1215.

Henry and Eleanor took no notice, Louis considered their defiance to be treason and he prepared for war. However, the speed and force of Henry's counterattacks quickly led him to beg for a truce. He was no match for Eleanor's new husband.

Henry was in no mood to trifle with Louis. Henry's main preoccupation was to invade England and take the kingdom from King Stephen. Stephen was the man who had seized the throne from Henry's mother, Matilda. In January 1153, he set sail for England from the port of Barfleur in Normandy. With him was an invading army of over 3,000 men.

England had been suffering from a civil war for almost nineteen years and people were longing for a strong government. Henry knew that he would be welcomed by most of the English barons—except, of course, for Stephen's son Eustace, who would naturally resist him.

In July 1153, after capturing many English towns and castles, Henry met Stephen's forces at Wallingford Castle, near Oxford. The archbishop of Canterbury and many of the barons urged the two sides to negotiate. However, two events suddenly changed things. First, Stephen's son Eustace became sick and died of food poisoning. Second, news came from Poitiers that Eleanor had just given birth to a son. Oddly enough, these two events had taken place on the very same day.

With Eustace dead, Stephen and Henry met at Winchester, England's former Saxon capital, and negotiated a settlement. Winchester was England's former Saxon capital. They decided that Stephen would remain king for the rest of his life and Henry would be his successor. As it turned out, Stephen would live for less than a year. He died of acute appendicitis in October 1154. He was fifty-seven years old. Henry, delighted by this turn of events, was able to claim the throne of England. And naturally, he was eager to bring Eleanor to Westminster Abbey in London so that they could be crowned together.

THE SPECTACULAR CORONATION OF THE KING AND QUEEN OF ENGLAND

When Eleanor and Henry arrived in England, they were given the most magnificent coronation that had ever taken place in London. Never before in England had anyone witnessed such gorgeous clothes as those worn by Eleanor. Her dress, which was from Constantinople, consisted of a tight-fitting robe of gold cloth. Over this shimmering garment hung a royal cloak of violet silk. The cloak was richly embroidered with gold fleur-de-lys (the emblem of France) and leopards (the emblem of England at the time). It was also edged with ermine. Eleanor's head-dress was formed of bands of gold, with huge pearls, rubies, and emeralds. Her hair, which was braided and coiled around her head, was loosely covered with an oriental veil of silver tissue.

At that time, men's fashions called for long hair. However, Henry shocked many of those present with his closely cropped red hair. He had a bristling moustache and a clean-shaven chin, defying the fashion for beards. He too was finely dressed, wearing his distinctive short cloak. It's possible that it was at this time that Henry earned the nickname of "Curtmantle" (short cloak).

To add extra splendor to the occasion, Eleanor insisted that the archbishop and clergy wear velvet and silk ceremonial garments. These were heavily embroidered with gold thread. Never before had clergymen in the West worn such fine clothes. Eleanor had admired the elaborately decorated robes of the Greek priests she had seen in Byzantium and the Holy Land, and she felt that it was time that similar rich vestments be worn in the western European church.

With this display of riches, England was demonstrating a new confidence. At age twenty-one, Henry

This twelfth-century manuscript illustration of a royal wedding gives us an example of the type of fashionable clothing that Eleanor and Henry wore. The bride *(second from left)* is dressed in extremely fitted clothing. She is holding down the cord that fastens her cloak together. She is also wearing her hair loose, which is a symbol of virginity and the unmarried state. The woman on the left is possibly the mother of the bride. The man on the far right is the groom. The man second from the right may be the father of the bride or groom.

was now the most powerful ruler in Europe. His empire stretched from the Scottish border in the north to the mountains of Spain in the south. It was an enormous expanse of territory with lands along each side of the English Channel. It would need someone with exceptional energy, strength, and organizational skills to defend it. Luckily, Henry was just such a king.

ELEANOR AND HENRY BEGIN THEIR RULE

England had been in a state of chaos for years, but Henry, who was extremely determined, forced law and order upon his new kingdom. He strengthened the legal system by appointing professional judges and introducing the jury system. He also imposed fair taxes and ruthlessly confined the power of the unruly barons by physically knocking down their castles.

He was constantly on the move. He kept a watchful eye over his vast territories and insisted that fresh horses were always kept ready for his use in abbeys all over the country. (When he arrived anywhere, his horses were exhausted, so he needed new ones to continue his journey.) No one knew when he would make his sudden appearance. He seemed to be everywhere at once. Eleanor soon realized that

THE PLANTAGENET DYNASTY

The Plantagenets, a new dynasty, came to the throne of England when Henry II became king. They remained in power for 331 years, until the Battle of Bosworth in 1485. After the battle, the Tudors took over. The name "Plantagenet" comes from the fact that Count Geoffrey, Henry's father, used to wear a yellow broom flower on his helmet as an identifying emblem. The Latin name for broom flower is *planta genista.*

her second husband appeared to have superhuman energy. He wasted no time over meals, which he usually ate standing up. No one ever dared to contradict him, as his temper was legendary.

In many respects, Eleanor was a perfect queen for such a man. She, too, had an amazing amount of energy. She frequently went with Henry on his journeys, both in England and in France. Eleanor was a natural commander; when she did not accompany Henry, he often left her in charge of governing the country. She was constantly traveling to visit her own vassals in Poitou and Aquitaine. She also made regular visits to abbeys and nunneries throughout their empire, usually donating generous gifts to them. She dressed herself magnificently, especially at the ceremonies known as crown-wearings. These special royal assemblies of the greatest nobles and their ladies were held at Christmas and Easter. At these events, which were usually held in Westminster or Winchester, the king and queen wore their crowns as symbols of royal authority.

Because of her constant need to travel around her large empire, Eleanor had palaces and great castles available to her in many cities throughout England. When she was in London, her main place of residence was the Tower of London. The tower had originally been built by William the Conqueror. During their reign, Henry also enlarged and rebuilt Windsor Castle, which is still one of England's royal homes. Other important palaces were at Winchester, Woodstock, and Oxford. And of course, Eleanor brought her personal luxuries to decorate them.

It was a busy, happy, and successful time for Eleanor. Amid all the responsibilities, ceremonial duties, and constant traveling, she fulfilled the duty of every queen by producing son after son, thus ensuring a plentiful supply of heirs.

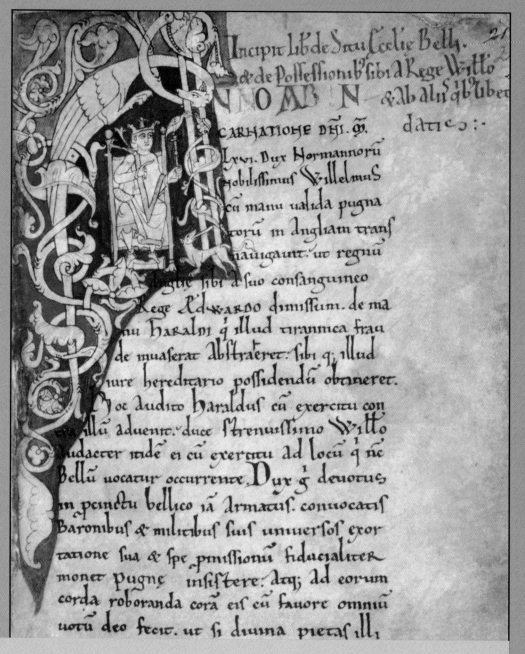

This English illuminated manuscript page from *The Chronicle of Battle Abbey* (circa 1155) features King William the Conqueror sitting on a throne in the upper left-hand corner of the page. The chronicle was written at Battle Abbey, which was the site of the Battle of Hastings. In the year 1066, William (who was then the Duke of Normandy) invaded England and took over the English throne after having triumphed over King Harold at the Battle of Hastings. It was after this that he became known as William the Conquerer.

The first child, William—who was born in 1153—did not survive long. He died in 1156. But then another birth came almost every year—making seven survivors in all. There was Henry, in 1155; Matilda, in 1156; Richard (later to become King Richard the Lionheart), in 1157; Geoffrey, in 1158; Eleanor, in 1161; Joan, in 1165; and finally, their last baby, John (who would become famous as the king who signed the Magna Carta), born in 1166.

RICHARD THE LIONHEART

King Richard I, the son of King Henry II, succeeded his father as king of England. He was a very capable military commander. He personally led his troops into battle on many occasions. In fact, his whole life was spent fighting or practicing military skills. His immense bravery led to him being nicknamed Richard Coeur de Lion, or in English, Richard the Lionheart.

Eleanor already had two daughters by her first husband, King Louis. At the age of forty-four, Eleanor could look back on an extremely eventful life. Little did she know, however, that her most important years were still to come.

FAMILY PROBLEMS

CHAPTER 5

Family matters now played an increasingly important part in Eleanor's life. The years that followed the birth of her last child were eventful and turbulent. This was particularly because her four sons—Henry, Richard, Geoffrey, and John—were growing older. Like Eleanor and Henry, all four sons were extremely active and had immense pride and ambition. They also constantly quarreled with one another, and with their father. The three eldest, Henry, Richard, and Geoffrey, were close in age. However, John, the youngest (eleven years younger than Henry), was always conscious that he was looked down upon as the little brother.

In 1169, Henry II declared how he intended to divide his empire after his death. Accompanied by his sons Henry and Richard, Henry II met King Louis

This illuminated manuscript page shows portraits of Henry II *(top left)* and his two sons who would later become kings, Richard I *(top right)* pictured with a sword, and John I *(bottom left)* who succeeded Richard as king. Richard, who was known as Richard the Lionheart for his bravery in battle, is pictured holding a sword and a shield—symbols of the courage and fierceness of a great warrior. The churches or abbeys behind Henry II and John may represent churches that these monarchs built or endowed.

of France at the castle of Montmirail in northern France. The result of the encounter, the Treaty of Montmirail, specified that young Prince Henry would inherit England, Normandy, and Anjou; Prince Richard would inherit Aquitaine as a vassal of the king of France; and Prince Geoffrey would receive Brittany as a vassal of his brother Henry.

Furthermore, Richard was to become engaged to Alys, then age nine. Alys was the daughter of King Louis and his second wife. She was to be placed immediately in the care of King Henry II in England. Under the terms of this treaty, Prince John, age three, was to receive nothing at all. Even at that young age, Henry II and Eleanor planned a career for him in the church. Jokingly, Henry gave John the curious nickname "Lackland," and this name stuck for many years.

The daughters of Eleanor and Henry did not receive anything either. This was because they were expected to marry into other noble families. And, in the course of time, they did so. Matilda married the Duke of Saxony and Bavaria and had ten children; Eleanor married the king of Castile and had twelve children; and Joan married the king of Sicily and had three children. In all, Eleanor and Henry would have thirty-five grandchildren.

HENRY THE YOUNG KING

Serious troubles began for Henry II in 1170, when he decided that it would be useful to crown his eldest son king. The strange custom of crowning an heir to the throne in the lifetime of his father had long been a common practice in France. The theory behind it was to enable a smooth succession in case the king died suddenly. Having a "spare" king already crowned prevented anyone else from trying to take the throne.

Accordingly, a coronation service took place on June 14, 1170, in London's Westminster Abbey. At age fifteen, Henry the Young King, as he was now to be called—was crowned. He was given the titles of king of England, Duke of Normandy, and Count of Anjou.

Henry the Young King was physically powerful and skilled in the arts of jousting and warfare. However, several historians of the time who knew him well wrote biting comments about his character. For example, in his *Chronicles of the Reigns of Stephen, Henry II and Richard I,* which was written in the mid-twelfth century, the abbot of Mont Saint Michel, Robert of Torigni, called Henry "weak, vain, idle [lazy], untrustworthy, and an irresponsible spendthrift [a big spender]." Walter Map, one of

This photo shows a part of the choir in the famous Westminster Abbey in London. Originally, the choir was the part of the abbey in which the monks prayed. The monks wore the black habit of the Order of Saint Benedict, who established the Benedictine rules for monks in his own abbey at Monte Cassino in Italy in about 540. Westminster Abbey has been the setting of every coronation that has taken place in England since the year 1066, when on December 25, William the Conquerer became king. More than 100 years later, the Young King was crowned in this same building.

Henry II's advisers, wrote of Henry II's violent temper in his book *Courtiers' Trifles* (circa 1181–1192). Even at his coronation, he was incredibly rude to his father, Henry II, who, luckily for him, was ready to overlook the incident.

Almost immediately after his coronation, the Young King started to provoke his father, asking for privileges to go with his title. For example, he asked to be allowed to share in the governing of England, or, failing that, to rule Normandy or Anjou. However, Henry II had no intention of letting any power get into the hands of the ambitious youngster. Furthermore, he made sure that the Young King was not given too much money since he was so careless with it.

Eleanor had not been present at Henry the Young King's coronation. The busy lifestyle she and Henry II lead meant that she was living more and more apart from her husband. At the time of the coronation of the Young King, Eleanor had gone to Poitiers for a ceremony in which her twelve-year-old son Richard (the future King Richard the Lionheart) was formally given the title of Count of Poitou. It seemed that Richard was Eleanor's favorite child. She was eager to introduce him to her subjects in Poitou and Aquitaine as their future duke. Meanwhile, in Rennes Cathedral, in the north of France, the youngest of the three heirs to Henry's estate, ten-year-old Geoffrey, had been proclaimed Duke of Brittany.

With all these preparations completed, Henry II felt safe that the future of his territories was secure. Unfortunately for him, however, the coronation of Henry the Young King triggered a sequence of events that would shake all of Europe.

le pere car il estoit ia malade ⁊ seru de pralisie
sitome listoure dieu cy apres plus plamement.
Er fine listoire du roy loys filz au roy loys le gros.

Cy commencent les croniques ⁊ histoires du
Roy philipe dieu donne filz au bon roy loys pre
mierement deuise comment ⁊ en quelle mani
ere il fu nez Et de laduision son pere precedas
En lan de lincarnacion mil cent
soixante ⁊ cinq fu nez le bon roy
philipe dieu donne en long zies
me kalende de septembre a la
feste saint thymothe ⁊ saint
mmphorien. Quant lenfant fu nez il fiap

KING HENRY II AND THOMAS BECKET

Earlier in his reign, Henry II had enjoyed the friendship and services of an extremely capable courtier named Thomas Becket. Becket was a man of humble origins whom Henry II had swiftly promoted to chancellor of England. He was Henry's chief political adviser and his right-hand man in governing the country. The relationship between the two was going well until the king decided that Becket would be just the man to fill the vacant post of archbishop of Canterbury. He thought that if Becket became the head of the church, he would help to bring the bishops and clergy under the rule of the king. All priests owed obedience primarily to the pope in Rome, but Henry demanded that their obedience should be to him first. He expected Becket to carry out his orders just as he had done when he was chancellor.

However, to Henry's surprise and annoyance, Thomas Becket immediately behaved as if the king

The coronation of Henry the Young King would have been similar to what is depicted here, in this illuminated manuscript page from *Les Grandes Chroniques de France*. In this image, Philip Auguste II, king of France *(pictured kneeling)*, is being crowned in the Cathedral of Reims in the presence of the Duke of Normandy, who was the son of King Henry II of England.

had no authority in church matters. He argued that a mere king could not interfere with the rights of priests. Henry and Becket disagreed so strongly that eventually, Becket decided to flee to the European continent, in order to give them time to let their anger die down.

It was while Thomas Becket was in self-imposed exile that Henry had decided to hold the coronation of the Young King. However, according to the traditions and teaching of the church, the only person in England who could crown the Young King was the archbishop of Canterbury, Thomas Becket.

Becket was furious that the coronation was going ahead without him. He sent word to the king, ordering him not to proceed with this coronation. Becket also threatened the king with excommunication if he did. The pope also sent Henry a letter forbidding the coronation.

This is a thirteenth-century British illuminated manuscript page featuring a depiction of the assassination of Thomas Becket. Becket was the archbishop of Canterbury and the chancellor of Henry II. On December 29, 1170, Becket was murdered in confusing circumstances by loyalist knights. He immediately became a martyr. Once he was dead, his body was removed and placed in the shrine before the altar of Christ. The following day, he was carried by monks who placed his corpse in a marble tomb in the crypt.

The situation was explosive. Eleanor's crucial role, of her own initiative, was to close the French ports, thus temporarily forbidding any ship to make the passage to England. This made it impossible for the pope's message to cross the English Channel.

BECKET AND KING HENRY'S VIOLENT TEMPER

After the coronation had taken place, Becket was allowed back into England, though he was still angry with the bishops who had taken part in crowning the Young King. In order to make a large impact on the members of his congregation, Becket chose the important occasion of his Christmas Day sermon in Canterbury Cathedral to pronounce the sentence of excommunication on them all. Privately, he was heard to exclaim (according to John of Salisbury, Becket's private secretary) that he would "tear the crown from the Young King's head!"

When King Henry heard that Becket had excommunicated the bishops, he exploded with rage. According to historians, he is reported to have shouted out to everyone within hearing distance, "Will no one rid me of this turbulent [troublesome] priest?" Recognizing the anger in Henry's voice, four knights galloped off to do what they thought the king wanted them to do. They murdered Becket within his own cathedral.

It is impossible to exaggerate the shock and horror felt throughout Europe at this bloody assassination of an archbishop in his own cathedral. Henry II was devastated by the consequences of his words. He had not intended anyone to take them literally. He made public penance in Canterbury Cathedral for his part in Becket's death. Despite this, he was hated and despised throughout the Christian world. Becket was declared by the pope to be a saint within three years of his death.

Eleanor must have shared the horror over Becket's murder, and this may well have turned her against her husband. She had supported Henry II during the quarrel itself, but she could hardly have foreseen its terrible consequences. Partly as a result of this, Eleanor and Henry drifted further and further apart. But there were other, more personal reasons why their relationship was becoming strained.

REBELLION, IMPRISONMENT, AND THE DEATH OF HENRY

1
2
3
4
5

7
8

CHAPTER 6

The marriage between Eleanor and Henry II was already going poorly because of a scandalous affair Henry was having with his mistress, Rosamund Clifford, known as Fair Rosamund.

According to historians, the affair started around 1165 and continued, at first secretly and then openly, until Rosamund's death in 1176. Rumors circulated about how Henry had built a secret hideout for Rosamund in the middle of a labyrinth at the royal palace at Woodstock. The rumors became more and more inventive.

For centuries afterward, stories were written about how Eleanor traced a way through this maze, following the end of a ball of wool that had accidentally attached itself to Henry's clothing. According to these fables, when Eleanor finally discovered

Rosamund, she gave her the option of taking poison or being stabbed to death.

Aside from Rosamund, Henry had affairs with many other women. He had at least twelve illegitimate children by various women, one of whom, Geoffrey, became an archbishop of York. Another, William Longespée, became the Earl of Salisbury. People were most shocked when Henry had an illegitimate son by Alys, who was the daughter of King Louis of France—and who was engaged to Henry's son, Richard. Alys had been entrusted to Henry and Eleanor's care since she was nine years old.

This is the great seal of Henry II. The seal would have been attached to documents Henry wrote or looked at. This would indicate that he agreed or signed off on what was written. Otherwise, fake documents could have been easily prepared in his name. On the seal, King Henry is shown seated on his throne.

ELEANOR SUPPORTS HER SONS AGAINST HENRY

Meanwhile, Henry the Young King was constantly asking his father for at least a part of his inheritance. He had an empty title, with no power, land, or responsibility. Every time he raised the subject, King Henry flew into a rage and told him not to be rude. The Young King was particularly angry when Henry II promised to give Prince John three castles in France and some English estates—all of which had already been promised to Henry the Young King.

Because of this treatment, Henry the Young King developed a savage hatred of his father. By then, he had married Marguerite of France, daughter of King Louis VII of France by his second wife. It is not surprising that the Young King turned to his father-in-law, Louis, for support. Louis was only too ready to side with the rebellious Henry the Young King against Henry II.

Eleanor and Louis, together with the three brothers, Henry the Young King, Richard, and Geoffrey, were actively plotting against Henry II. John was still too young and inexperienced in warfare to join them. The three brothers were in Paris gathering troops and supporters to fight for the lands they regarded as their rightful possessions. Meanwhile, Louis and his

This photo shows what houses look like in the old town of Rouen, where it is possible that Eleanor was taken prisoner by King Henry. Rouen, which is located in the French department of Seine-Maritime, is particularly famous for being the site of the trial of Joan of Arc, the famous heroine of France. The capital of upper Normandy, Rouen first became famous when the Romans chose the region as their capital. They named it Rothomagas.

nobles were offering their support against King Henry II. Eleanor was making her way from Poitiers to join them in Paris. As she was undertaking the journey in great secrecy, she dressed as a man. Unfortunately for her, however, her husband had his spies well trained. Her party was suddenly ambushed and Eleanor was taken prisoner.

ELEANOR IS IMPRISONED

It is not known where Eleanor was first imprisoned, as King Henry made no announcement that she was

FONTEVRAULT ABBEY

During the Middle Ages, Fontevrault Abbey in France was an exceptionally important nunnery. It was used as a home for royal and noble-born ladies in their retirement. Eleanor gave generously toward its upkeep and frequently visited it whenever she was in that area of France. After their deaths, Henry II, Eleanor, and Richard I were buried there. Many tourists visit Fontevrault to see their magnificent tombs.

his captive. She may have been taken to a fortress in Rouen or perhaps to the castle at Falaise, where William the Conqueror had been born. Wherever it was, Eleanor disappeared from public view for at least a year. In his book *Concerning Instruction of Princes*, written circa 1176, a historian named Gerald of Wales (circa 1146–1220), wrote that Henry II "imprisoned Queen Eleanor his wife as a punishment for the destruction of their marriage."

As for the uprising, King Henry soon proved more than a match for his rebellious sons and the armies of King Louis. He defeated them and the young princes promised not to disobey him again. He forgave them, excusing them because they were still

This page from a fourteenth-century French illuminated manuscript shows nuns praying and receiving
confession. Because they are wearing black habits, it's
possible that they are Benedictine nuns. These were
probably upper-class women who weren't married
and as a consequence, entered a religious order. This
was very common for women who were not able or
willing to find partners in marriage. Sometimes they
chose to enter religious orders, but many were not
given the choice and were forced to enter.

young. As for Eleanor, however, he would keep her prisoner for the rest of his life.

Eleanor spent most of her imprisonment at Winchester, the ancient Saxon capital of England, about 60 miles (96 kilometers) west of London. Although she was fairly comfortable, her movements were restricted, and her family was not allowed to visit her. Sometimes she was moved to another castle, at the city of Sarum, 25 miles (40 km) west of Winchester. She was far less comfortable there because of its location in a small, bleak, and windswept fortress on a hill. Eleanor was completely cut off from the rest of the world. After all, in Sarum, even water was a luxury.

In far-off Poitou and Aquitaine, Eleanor's subjects grieved for the loss of their duchess. Meanwhile, her son Richard was governing these provinces in her absence. As for Henry, he was now living openly with his mistress, Rosamund Clifford. When the pope refused to grant his request for a divorce, Henry tried to make Eleanor agree to become abbess at the Fontevrault Abbey in France. She refused. This would force her to live a life of retirement. She would be completely cut off from society, and would have nothing to do but pray. Eleanor considered being forced to become a nun to be just as bad as being imprisoned against her will.

HENRY II'S FINAL YEARS

The months and years dragged on. Rosamund died in 1176. It was at this time that Henry took his sixteen-year-old stepdaughter, Alys, as his mistress. As for Henry the Young King, he was becoming extremely frustrated. This was especially due to the fact that his brothers were now being given real responsibilities in governing their lands while he— the king of England in name only—was left doing nothing but exercising his skills at jousting.

However, in the following years, the political situation changed considerably. In 1179, King Louis of France died after suffering a stroke, and his fourteen-year-old son Philip became king. Then, in 1183, at age twenty-eight, Henry the Young King fell ill with a severe form of diarrhea known as dysentery and died. On his deathbed, he sent a message to his father, begging him to show mercy to his mother. When Eleanor, who was still being held at Sarum Castle, heard of his death, she was very sad. However, she realized that this was good news for her favorite son, Richard, who was now heir to Henry's enormous empire.

At this point, Eleanor, age sixty-one, had been captive for ten years. Now that the dangerous Young King was out of the way, Henry II was prepared to allow her to appear in public on special occasions, though she would still be closely guarded. The problem now facing Henry II was how to redistribute his territories among his remaining sons. By this time, John, the youngest, was an adult. As was natural, he expected some part of the empire for himself.

Henry proposed giving Aquitaine to John, but not surprisingly, Richard was outraged at the thought of having his province taken from him. He quickly joined forces with Philip, the new king of France. Eventually, after a few years, full-scale war broke out between Henry and his son Richard. King Philip of France was siding with Richard, and even John—who had until then been considered to be on his father's side—also turned against his father. However, for a while Henry did not know of John's treachery.

By 1189, Henry was weary, old, and ill. When he learned that John had conspired against him, he was tormented by the thought of his son's disloyalty. After capturing many of Henry's castles and towns, King Philip, aided by Richard and John, forced Henry to surrender. In his sickness, Henry had no option but to acknowledge defeat. According to the book *Concerning the Instruction of Princes* by the king's personal chaplain, Gerald of Wales, Henry's last words were: "Shame, shame on a conquered king."

This is a detail of an illuminated manuscript page with a double image featuring Henry II. The upper portion of the illustration shows Henry on his deathbed. The lower half shows a scribe writing the will that Henry is dictating.

King Henry II died on July 6, 1189, at his castle at Chinon, near the Loire Valley. Richard became king of England. Not surprisingly, one of the first acts of his reign was to order that his mother, Eleanor, be immediately released from prison.

ELEANOR RULES ENGLAND FOR RICHARD THE LIONHEART

When he became king, Richard was thirty-one years old, strikingly handsome, broad-shouldered, strong, and over six feet tall (1.8 meters). Above all, he adored every aspect of warfare; he was utterly fearless in battle and a natural leader of men. Though still unmarried, he was engaged to Alys, the sister of King Philip of France. He had inherited Eleanor's good looks and his father's ferocious temper. Most of the time he was friendly, courteous, and easy-going. Like Eleanor, he loved music and poetry. He wrote songs in the style of the troubadours of his native Aquitaine.

Richard hurried to Chinon to see his dead father and to organize the funeral at Fontevrault Abbey. He had sent letters to England to order Eleanor's release. However, he also authorized her to act as his deputy and rule England until he could arrive there himself. The messenger found that news of Henry's death had already reached Winchester and Eleanor was enjoying her freedom. She had set up a royal court and was receiving visitors. She had also taken the reins of government into her hands.

Eleanor was now sixty-seven and had lived in captivity for fifteen years. She emerged from her long period of imprisonment with immense energy, authority, dignity, and wisdom. Like Richard, she too was a natural leader. She relished the power that Richard had given her.

Eleanor knew Richard wouldn't arrive in England for some time, so she toured southern England acting on Richard's behalf. She dispensed justice, settled disputes, received homage, and made everyone swear obedience to the new king. She passed new laws concerning weights and measures, decreed that a new coinage should be minted, and released prisoners who had been wrongfully treated. Eleanor also canceled some of Henry's unpopular laws and announced that it was no longer necessary for abbeys throughout the land to keep horses at the ready for use by the king.

It was a whirlwind of activity and she impressed everyone with her grasp of what needed to be done as well as the wisdom of her judgments.

She then placed Alys under guard in Winchester castle. Clearly, she did not intend that Alys's marriage to Richard should take place.

When Richard arrived in England, he was met by Eleanor and his brother John. Together, they traveled through the kingdom to Windsor. He was to be crowned at Westminster Abbey in September. Meanwhile, John married his wealthy cousin Hawise of Gloucester. As a wedding present, Richard gave him six English counties and some land in France. He was also put in charge of Ireland.

Richard's coronation was a wonderful affair. However, although he was king, he had no interest in governing England. Instead, he was totally absorbed by an exciting challenge that had just presented itself—another crusade, this one called the Third Crusade. From now on, his main interest would be to raise enough money from taxing the English subjects to meet the expenses of going to the Holy Land.

RICHARD LEAVES ENGLAND IN ELEANOR'S CARE

Jerusalem had been captured by the Muslim leader, Saladin, and Richard and King Philip of France were

This fifteenth-century French illuminated manuscript called *Le Premier Volume des Anciennes et Nouvelles Chroniques d'Angleterre* (The First Volume of Ancient and New Chronicles of England) illustrates the coronation procession of Richard I, king of England.

Richard I, also called the Lionheart, was the third son of King Henry II and Eleanor of Aquitaine. He was born on September 8, 1157, at Beaumont Palace in Oxford. He died on April 6, 1199, in Aquitaine. Soon after his coronation, he prepared to fight in the Third Crusade.

enthusiastic about taking up the pope's call to arms to liberate that holy city. Richard quickly sold everything he could. To gather more money, he raised taxes for his great project. Having made all the necessary preparations, Richard set off with his army to join forces with King Philip in July 1190. He left two deputies in charge of running his affairs in England. Nonetheless, it was clearly understood that both men were subject to the ultimate authority of Eleanor. At this point, she was now England's monarch in all but name. Richard's brother John was given no power at all.

Eleanor was most concerned with the problem of Richard's marriage. By then, Alys was imprisoned in Rouen. Neither Eleanor nor Richard wanted anything to do with her after her affair with the late King Henry. Secretly, they made a plan. As soon as Richard had left England for the Holy Land, Eleanor would go to Navarre, a small kingdom in the Pyrenees between France and Spain. They had already negotiated that Richard would marry Berengaria, the eldest daughter of King Sancho of Navarre. The plan was that Eleanor would then bring Berengaria to wherever Richard was, and Richard would marry her as soon as possible. The difficulty was, of course, that King Philip of France,

RICHARD AND BERENGARIA

On their way to rejoin Philip in the Holy Land, Richard and Berengaria were married in Limassol, Cyprus. Berengaria then accompanied Richard during his crusade. Afterward, she set off for England without Richard. However, she preferred Aquitaine and ended up staying there. They never had children and met only rarely during their eight-year marriage. After Richard's death, Berengaria founded an abbey in L'Epau, France, where she lived as a nun, helping the poor and the sick.

Alys's brother, would be furious when he found out about this alternative bride for Richard.

Despite her age and the difficulty and length of the journey, Eleanor succeeded in traveling to Navarre. She then made the final marriage negotiations. Next, Eleanor brought Berengaria to Sicily, where Richard and Philip had met up with one another. As expected, Philip exploded with anger when Eleanor arrived with Berengaria. Although both kings were still committed to liberating Jerusalem, it was clear that their former close

This illuminated manuscript page showing a joust between a crusader and a Muslim is believed to be a depiction of a fight between King Richard the Lionheart and the Sultan Saladin. Saladin, an excellent military strategist as well as one of the most famous Muslim heroes, was born in 1138 in Tikrit (Mesopotamia) in Iraq. Saladin was the son of a Kurdish chief named Ayyub. The manuscript was written circa 1340 by Sir Geoffrey Luttrell of Irnham.

friendship was over. Still angry with Richard, Philip departed ahead of him. He left with his army for the Holy Land.

DIFFICULTIES FOR RICHARD

When Richard arrived in the Holy Land, he joined forces with Philip of France and with Duke Leopold of Austria. Leopold had also brought his small army to

fight in the crusade. Unfortunately, after the combined armies had captured the city of Acre, Richard's men made Leopold extremely angry. He was furious when his Austrian flags of victory—which were flying alongside those of Richard and Philip—were torn down and trampled on by English soldiers. It was an insult that Leopold could not forgive. He returned home to Austria, feeling deeply humiliated.

King Philip of France also returned home, leaving Richard to continue the crusade alone with his English troops. Richard fought and won many battles, but in the end, he did not succeed in liberating Jerusalem. Nevertheless, he did achieve a negotiated settlement with his Muslim opponent, Saladin. They agreed that

This is a fresco showing a group of pilgrims entering a church. The church probably contained a saint's shrine, the object of their journey. A fresco is a type of painting in which water-based pigments are applied or painted onto freshly plastered walls or canvas. Many medieval frescoes were quite crudely painted. However, later artists became very skilled. The finest examples of fresco painting can be found in the Sistine Chapel in Rome, painted by Michelangelo.

Christian pilgrims were to be allowed safe passage to visit Jerusalem. This agreement lasted for many years and was much appreciated by the Christian pilgrims.

Eleanor had not accompanied Richard to the Holy Land. After delivering Berengaria to Richard in Sicily, she received news that her youngest son, John, was creating trouble back in England. He was seizing power for himself and posing a danger to Richard. John was claiming to be Richard's heir and was spreading the false rumor that Richard would not be returning to England. Worse still, when Philip got back to France, John quickly made friends with him, and promised to give him all of Richard's continental possessions if he helped him become king of England.

In the face of this threat to Richard, Eleanor traveled to various cities in England. At each stop, she summoned meetings of the English nobles and clergy who lived nearby to make them renew their oaths of obedience to Richard. She used her authority as Richard's deputy to rule England as its queen, and in order to restrain John, she made him promise not to go to France to join up with Philip. She threatened to confiscate all of John's English property if he disobeyed her. In his book *Images of History* (circa 1201), historian Ralph de Diceto, who lived at this time, wrote: "Eleanor, the King's mother, did her utmost to conserve the peace of the kingdom." Another medieval writer, Matthew Paris, in *History of the English* (written circa 1253), described how Eleanor was "exceedingly respected and beloved." Paris noted that she ruled the country "with great wisdom and popularity."

RICHARD IS CAPTURED

Early in 1193, some startling news arrived from Austria. On his way back from the Holy Land, Richard

This twelfth-century illustration depicts the capture of Richard the Lionheart *(top)*, as well as Richard paying homage to Holy Roman Emperor Henry VI *(bottom)*. The title of emperor was given to a succession of German kings who were regarded as chief of all European kings. After the sixteenth century, the title became merely an honor. There was no power associated with it.

had been captured by Leopold of Austria. The news delighted John, who immediately went to Paris. Philip welcomed him and offered to do whatever he could to help him become king of England. Meanwhile, Eleanor felt she should return to London to settle matters.

Further news arrived. Leopold had handed Richard over to the Holy Roman Emperor Henry VI. He was demanding 100,000 silver marks from England as ransom money for their king. This was the equivalent of twice England's total annual revenue—a huge sum—and it was up to Eleanor to meet this demand.

Eleanor immediately set about collecting the required ransom money. She ordered that every man in England give up one quarter of his income. Poor people had to give what they could—pigs were killed, sheep shorn, and churches were stripped of their valuables. Eleanor appointed five noblemen to oversee all this work. As the money came in, it was stored in big wooden chests in Old St. Paul's Cathedral in London.

Eventually, over thirty-five tons of silver were passed over to the emperor, and on February 4, 1194, Richard was finally released. Eleanor traveled to Germany to greet her son. Crying tears of joy, she broke down as the royal prisoner was handed over to her. Then, she and Richard began the long journey

Peasants depended on their livestock (sheep, cows, chickens, and goats) for food and income. This illuminated manuscript page from a Book of Hours shows a man shearing a sheep. This late fifteenth-century Flemish Book of Hours contained an illustration for each month. This image represents June. (A Book of Hours is a prayer book containing prayers to be said at special times of the day.)

back home to England. Clearly, there was much to discuss and vital business to attend to.

On March 12, 1194, they landed at the south coast of England. They immediately made their way to Canterbury, where they gave thanks to God at the newly built shrine of Saint Thomas Becket.

ELEANOR'S EXCITING FINAL YEARS

To celebrate his homecoming in April 1194, Richard was given a second coronation. This time it took place in Winchester Cathedral. During the event, Eleanor sat high up on a raised platform. From there, she watched her son with pride as he moved in procession with the archbishops of Canterbury and Dublin, together with a large gathering of earls, barons, and knights. The great ceremony was the result of Eleanor's efforts to restore dignity and power to her son. She was now seventy-two years old, and this was a great moment in her long, eventful life.

Less than a month after this second coronation, Richard and Eleanor left England to deal with matters in their continental possessions. Foremost in their minds was what to do with John, who was still plotting to take the throne.

A historian of the time, Richard of Hoveden, in his book *The Deeds of Henry II and the Deeds of Richard I* (circa 1200), wrote that on Richard's release, King Philip had sent an urgent warning to John stating, "Look to yourself. The Devil is loosed!" John immediately fled to Paris to be under Philip's protection.

With Richard firmly back on the throne, John was desperate to be forgiven. Shamefaced, he came to see Richard, and he begged Eleanor to help him. In *Images of History* by historian Ralph de Diceto, the author describes how John fell on his knees before Richard and tearfully asked for forgiveness. It says much for Richard's good nature that he raised John to his feet, saying, "Don't worry, you're just a child, and you were taken in by bad advisers." After this, John took care to keep well out of trouble for the rest of Richard's reign.

Richard needed to devote his energies to winning back the territories in France that Philip had captured from him during his long absence. The final five years of his reign were taken up with a constant series of battles against his bitter enemy Philip. Meanwhile, Eleanor had gone to Fontevrault Abbey, where she was living not as a nun but as a permanent, honored guest. She enjoyed making plans for her grandchildren. She decided to leave her lands in Poitou and Aquitaine to one of her grandsons, Otto of Saxony, who was the son of her daughter Matilda. Meanwhile, the future of Richard's possessions, and England in particular, must have given her some anxiety. This was because Richard still had no heir.

THE FATE OF RICHARD THE LIONHEART

In April 1199, devastating news came from Châlus, a little village near Limoges, about 100 miles (161 km) from Fontevrault. Richard had received a fatal wound from an arrow and was dying of gangrene.

As Richard had named his brother John as his successor, it became Eleanor's duty to make sure that her youngest son could take over this inheritance

This is a close-up view of the face of the tomb effigy of Richard the Lionheart, king of England. The twelfth-century tomb is made of multicolored stone. Richard, who had received a fatal wound in battle, had one final wish, which he told to his mother, Eleanor, after she rushed to his side. He wanted to be buried next to his father in Fontevrault, and he wanted his heart to be buried in Rouen Cathedral. Eleanor made it to her son's side just in time to see him take his last breath.

as smoothly as possible. Things were complicated, however, because she knew that there were many supporters of Arthur of Brittany who would oppose John's succession to the throne.

Arthur was the son of Eleanor's second son, Geoffrey, Duke of Brittany, who had died in 1186. At one time, Richard had actually named Arthur as his heir. However, because Arthur had become friends with King Philip, Richard had changed his mind. It was not surprising that Arthur was angry about this. It was certain that John could expect trouble from Arthur's supporters.

As expected, Arthur marched south from Britany with his army. His intention was to seize Poitou and wage war with John. Eleanor was furious at his treachery and set off with a military escort for Poitiers, the capital of Poitou. She hoped to prevent Arthur from capturing it. Unfortunately for her, Arthur learned her whereabouts and attacked the castle of Mirebeau, where she was staying. He hoped to capture her and hold her for ransom.

However, Eleanor held off his attacks. She managed to smuggle messengers out of the castle to tell John of her danger. On hearing the news, John quickly came to her rescue. With a surprise attack, he captured hundreds of Arthur's knights as well as Arthur himself. Arthur was thrown in prison and would never again be seen in public. With Eleanor's help, King John was able to crush this threat to his power.

ELEANOR'S LAST ROYAL DUTY

In 1199, John was crowned king in Westminster Abbey. Afterward, Eleanor, who was seventy-seven, undertook a 1,000-mile tour (1,600 km) of her possessions in Aquitaine. She busily attended to her affairs, settled disputes, made laws, granted charters, and brought order to her people. Her energy still seemed limitless.

Meanwhile, Philip and John decided to end the tension that had existed for so long between France and England. It suited them both to sign a five-year truce. John would pay 30,000 silver marks to Philip. In return, Philip would recognize John as Richard's heir. Part of the truce agreement was a proposed marriage between Philip's twelve-year-old son, Louis, and one of John's nieces. The niece to be chosen, a princess in Castile (present-day Spain), was one of Eleanor's many grandchildren.

Eleanor's last royal duty would be a happy one. She was to travel to Castile, choose a princess, and bring her back to France to marry Louis. It was an opportunity for Eleanor to see her daughter, also named Eleanor, for the first time in thirty years. The younger Eleanor had married the king of Castile. There were twelve children from this marriage, and Eleanor had never met any of them.

Eleanor traveled through the mountains of the Pyrenees in the wintertime. She arrived at the court of King Alfonso and Queen Eleanor of Castile in January 1200. Here, she met her grandchildren for the first time. Eleanor was a shrewd judge of character, and she chose Blanche, age sixteen, to marry Prince Louis. Time would prove the wisdom of her choice, for Blanche later became one of the greatest queens of France. Eleanor must have had memories of when she herself became queen of France at the same age.

Sadly, a disaster struck Eleanor's escort as they passed through Poitou on the way home. One of her faithful captains was killed in a brawl. The shock was almost too much for Eleanor. She handed Blanche over to the archbishop of Bordeaux, asking him to escort her to Paris. Eleanor then went back to Fontevrault, where she hoped to at last retire. At almost eighty years old, she needed some final years of peace. According to this wish, Eleanor was consecrated as a nun in 1202. Two years later, she died peacefully in her sleep.

This is another view of the tomb statue of Eleanor of Aquitaine, which is in the abbey church of Notre Dame de Fontevrault in France. Eleanor died on April 1, 1204.

Eleanor's tomb is still in Fontevrault Abbey, next to that of her husband Henry II and her son Richard I. A magnificent life-size stone carving shows Eleanor lying down, wearing a crown, and holding a prayer book. Upon her face is a gentle smile. Her many descendants would reign throughout Europe for centuries to come. Britain's present queen, Elizabeth II, is one of them.

At a time when women were regarded as the "weaker sex," Eleanor showed a natural ability as a ruler of men. In her early years, she was famed for her beauty, but as one of her contemporaries, Richard of Devizes, wrote in his book *Chronicles of the Times of King Richard the First* (circa 1190s), she was "an incomparable woman. Her power was the admiration of her age." Around 1152, a troubador poet named Bernard de Ventádour expressed his admiration for Eleanor with these lines:

> When the sweet breeze
> Blows hither from your dwelling
> Methinks I feel
> A breath of Paradise.

TIMELINE

circa 1122	Eleanor is born, probably at Poitiers or Bordeaux.
1137	At age fifteen, Eleanor becomes Duchess of Aquitaine. She marries Prince Louis and shortly after becomes queen of France.
1147–1149	Louis and Eleanor take part in the Second Crusade.
1152	Eleanor divorces Louis and marries Henry Plantagenet, Count of Anjou.
1154	Henry and Eleanor become king and queen of England.
1170	Thomas Becket, archbishop of Canterbury, is murdered.
1174–1189	Eleanor is imprisoned for plotting with her sons against Henry II.
1189	Henry II dies. Eleanor's son Richard becomes king. Eleanor is released and is given authority to be Richard's deputy.
1190–1191	Eleanor negotiates Richard's marriage to Berengaria of Navarre.
1191–1194	Eleanor rules England and raises money to pay the ransom of Richard, who is held prisoner by Holy Roman Emperor Henry VI.
1199	Richard I dies and is succeeded by King John. Eleanor helps to crush a rebellion against King John.
1200	Eleanor goes to Castile to arrange marriage negotiations between her granddaughter Blanche of Castile with Louis VIII of France. She retires to Fontevrault Abbey and becomes a nun.
1204	Eleanor dies and is buried at Fontevrault Abbey.

GLOSSARY

abbey A monastery, where monks live, work, and pray. The head of an abbey for men is called an abbot; the head of an abbey for women is called an abbess.

allegiance Loyalty given by a vassal to his king or lord.

annulment The legal termination of a marriage.

archbishop of Canterbury The most important clergyman in England.

Brittany A large province in north-west France.

Castile The name given in medieval times to the kingdom of Spain. This comes from the numerous castles that were built there.

chancellor In medieval England, the chancellor held the most important executive office in the kingdom, after the king himself. He enforced the king's command and was often given power to rule the country in the king's absence.

chaplain A priest employed by an individual to hold personal church services for his master or mistress.

count   A high-born nobleman, ranking just below a duke. A count ruled over a province that was called a county. His wife was called a countess.

Crusade   Between 1095 and 1271, there were nine crusades. These were holy wars undertaken by Christians who tried to capture Jerusalem from the Muslims. They were mostly unsuccessful. The name "crusade" comes from the cross that was worn on the tunics of the European armies.

duke, dukedom   A duke is a high-ranking noble-man, only one rank lower than a king. In the Middle Ages, dukes ruled provinces or large territories known as dukedoms. A duke's wife was called a duchess.

ermine   The white fur of a stoat. It was used to decorate royal and noble garments.

excommunicate   To banish or expel from the Catholic Church. Excommunication was considered a terrible punishment because those who were excommunicated were thought to go to hell when they died.

exile   Punishment by banishment from one's own home or country.

gangrene   Rotting flesh; a serious wound that becomes so infected that the affected flesh starts to die and rot away.

Holy Land   According to Christians, the land around Jerusalem where Jesus lived and died.

homage   A ceremony in which a vassal solemnly swears an oath of obedience to his superior lord or king.

illegitimate   Born from parents who are not married.

invested   To be given a title or an honor.

jousting   A medieval sport in which two knights on horseback carry lances (long pointed poles) with which they try to knock one another off their horses. This was considered good training for real warfare.

labyrinth   A maze or complicated pattern of paths that is specifically designed to confuse anyone trying to find a way out.

mark   A medieval coin equal in value to two-thirds of a pound but worth very much more than the present-day English pound.

martyrdom   Dying for one's religious faith. A martyr is one who suffers or dies for his or her beliefs.

maze   A complicated pattern of paths, deliberately made to confuse anyone who is trying to find his or her way to the object hidden in the middle; a labyrinth.

Muslim   A follower of the prophet Muhammad, believing in the faith of Islam.

Notre Dame   The cathedral at the center of Paris.

Old St. Paul's Cathedral   The cathedral in London that existed in the Middle Ages. It was burned down in 1666 and was replaced by the present St. Paul's Cathedral, which was built by the great British architect Sir Christopher Wren.

permissive   Having a relaxed attitude. A permissive society is one in which people feel free to do what they like (especially in sexual matters).

pilgrimage   A journey made to a sacred place or tomb of a saint. Many people during the Middle Ages made pilgrimages to offer prayers to the saints or holy people associated with those places.

shrine   A holy building or tomb of a saint, often elaborately decorated with precious stones and colored marble.

spendthrift   Someone who spends money unwisely, especially if that money has been saved carefully by someone else.

stoat   A small mammal of the weasel family. It eats rabbits and rodents and is good at climbing trees.

vassal   Someone who is dependent on a superior lord or king, and who owes loyalty and obedience to that lord.

For more information

WEB SITES
Due to the changing nature of internet links, the Rosen Publishing Group, Inc., has developed an online list of Web sites. These sites will be updated regularly. You can access the list at

http://www.rosenlinks.com/lema/elaq

FOR FURTHER READING

Hilliam, David. *Kings, Queens, Bones and Bastards.* Stroud, England: Sutton Publishing, 1998.

Meade, Marion. *Eleanor of Aquitaine: A Biography.* New York: Hawthorn, England: 1977.

Weir, Alison. *Eleanor of Aquitaine.* New York: Ballantine Books, 2000.

BIBLIOGRAPHY

Ashley, Maurice. *The Life and Times of King John*. London: Weidenfeld and Nicolson, 1972.

Gillingham, John. *The Life and Times of Richard I*. London: Weidenfeld and Nicolson, 1973,

Owen, D. D. R. *Eleanor of Aquitaine, Queen and Legend*. Oxford, England: Blackwell, 1993.

Pain, Nesta. *The King and Becket*. London: Eyre & Spottiswoode, 1964.

Schlight, John. *Henry II Plantagenet*. New York: Twayne, 1973.

Seward, Desmond. *Eleanor of Aquitaine: The Mother Queen*. London: Davids' Charles, 1978.

INDEX

A
Aigret, William (brother of Eleanor), 11, 13
Alix (daughter of Eleanor), 41
Alys (daughter of Louis VII), 56, 67, 73, 77, 79, 82–83
Anjou, 39, 42, 56, 57, 59
Antioch, 26, 31, 33, 34, 36, 37
Aquitaine, 8–10, 11, 14, 18, 19, 20, 22, 28, 38, 50, 56, 59, 72, 74, 77, 83, 92, 95

B
barons, 44
Becket, Thomas, 61–62, 64–65, 90
Berengaria (wife of Richard the Lionheart), 82–83, 86
Bernard of Clairvaux, 12, 22
Blanche (granddaughter of Eleanor), 96
Brittany, 56, 59, 94

C
Canterbury, 61, 62, 64, 65, 90, 91
Christianity, 12, 24, 26, 31, 32, 36, 65, 86
Clifford, Rosamund, 66–67, 72
Conrad, Emperor, 28, 29
Constantinople (Istanbul), 28, 29, 46
Crusades
First, 24, 26
Second, 7, 26–31, 32, 36
Third, 79–85

D
de Rançon, Geoffrey, 29, 31
Diceto, Ralph de, 87, 92
dukedoms of France, 7–9, 11

E
Edessa, 24, 26, 31, 32,
    33, 36
Eleanor (daughter of Eleanor
    of Aquitaine), 53, 56, 96
Eleanor of Aquitaine
    annulment of marriage to
        Louis, 41
    appearance of, 10, 14,
        16, 77, 98
    and the arts, 10, 15,
        20, 77
    children of, 26, 38, 41,
        46, 51–53
    death of, 96–97
    as Duchess of Aquitaine,
        18, 19, 42
    early life of, 11–19
    education of, 15–16
    and fashion, 14–15, 22,
        28, 32, 46–47
    imprisonment of, 69–72,
        73–74, 76, 77, 78
    marriage to Louis, 19
    meeting and marrying
        Henry, 40–41, 42–43
    as queen of England, 10,
        46–47, 50–51
    as queen of France, 10,
        19, 20–22, 28–41, 96
    relationship with

Raymond (uncle),
    32–33, 34
    ruling England for son
        Richard, 77–78, 82, 87
    and Second Crusade,
        27–31, 32, 36, 38
Elizabeth II, Queen, 97

F
Fontevrault Abbey, 70, 72,
    77, 92, 93, 96, 97

G
Gascony, 8, 11, 14, 18, 19
Geoffrey (son of Eleanor),
    53, 54, 59, 68, 94
Geoffrey of Anjou, Count,
    39, 42, 50
Gerald of Wales, 70, 76
Gervase of Canterbury, 28

H
Henry II, King
    and affairs, 66–67, 73, 82
    appearance of, 47
    becomes king of England,
        46–50
    death of, 74, 76, 77
    as Duke of Normandy, 39,
        40–41, 42–46
    imprisoning Eleanor,
        69–70, 72, 73–74
    meeting and marrying
        Eleanor, 40–41, 42–45
    relationship with
        sons, 53, 54–59,
        68–72, 74–76

and Thomas Becket,
61–65
tomb of, 70, 97
Henry the Young King; son
of Eleanor, 54, 56, 57–59,
68, 73
birth of, 53
coronation of, 62, 64
death of, 73
Henry VI, King, 89
Holy Land, 7, 24, 26, 79, 82,
83, 84, 86, 87
homage, ceremony of, 15

I

Innocent II, Pope, 12
Italy, 37

J

Jerusalem, 24, 26, 33,
34–36, 79, 83, 85–86
John, King (son of Eleanor),
56, 68, 74–76, 82
becomes king of England,
93–95
birth of, 53
and Magna Carta, 44, 53
marriage of, 79
plot to take throne,
86–87, 89, 91–92

L

Leopold of Austria, Duke,
84–85, 89
London, 46, 51, 57, 70, 89
Louis (son of King Philip),
95, 96

Louis VI, King, 17, 18–19, 22
Louis VII, King
annulment of marriage
to Eleanor, 41,43
becomes king of
France, 19
and burning of cathedral
of Vitry, 23–24
character of, 21, 22–23
children of, 53, 56, 67, 68
death of, 73
and Henry II, 39–40, 42,
43–45, 54–56, 68–70
marriage to Eleanor, 17,
18–19, 33–34, 36,
37–38
and religion, 21–22
and Second Crusade,
24–31, 32, 34–36, 38

M

Magna Carta, 44, 53
Matilda (daughter of
Eleanor), 53, 56, 93
Matilda (mother of Henry II),
39, 45
Muslims, 24, 26, 31, 36,
37, 79, 85

N

Normandy, 39, 40, 42, 45,
56, 57, 59
Notre Dame, 22
Nureddin, 37

O

Otto of Saxony, 92–93

P

Paris, 10, 19, 20, 22, 24, 38, 39, 42, 68, 69, 89, 96
Paris, Matthew, 87
Philip, King, 77, 95
  becomes king, 73, 74
  and Richard the
    Lionheart, 74, 76, 82–84, 87, 89, 92, 94
  and Third Crusade, 79–82, 85
Plantagenets, 50
Poitou, 8, 11, 14, 18, 19, 50, 72, 92, 94, 96

R

Raymond of Poitiers (uncle of Eleanor), 26, 31, 32–33, 34, 36, 37
Richard of Devizes, 98
Richard of Hoveden, 92
Richard the Lionheart, King (son of Eleanor), 68, 72, 73, 74, 86–87, 91–92, 95
  becomes king, 76, 77, 78–79
  birth of, 53
  capture and release of, 87–90, 92
  death of, 93–94
  early years, 54, 59, 67
  marriage of, 82–83

second coronation of, 91
and Third Crusade, 7, 79–82, 84–86
tomb of, 70, 97
Rome, 37, 61

S

Saladin, 79, 85
Stephen, King, 39, 45, 46
Suger, Abbot, 21–22, 26–27, 38

T

Tower of London, 51
Treaty of Montmirail, 56
Turks/Turkey, 24, 26, 28, 29, 30, 31, 32

V

Ventàdour, Bernard de, 98

W

Westminster Abbey, 46, 57, 79, 95
William IX, Duke of Aquitaine (grandfather of Eleanor), 11, 22
William X, Duke of Aquitaine (father of Eleanor), 7, 8, 11–14, 17–18, 32
William the Conqueror, 39, 51, 70

ABOUT THE AUTHOR

David Hilliam grew up in Salisbury and Winchester, England, and was educated at both Oxford and Cambridge Universities. He has taught at schools in Canterbury, London, and Versailles, France. He is passionately interested in the British monarchy. His books include *Kings, Queens, Bones and Bastards*; *Monarchs, Murders and Mistresses*; and his latest, *Crown Orb and Sceptre*, which is an account of all the British royal coronations. At present he lives and lectures in Dorset, England.

CREDITS

Designer: Evelyn Horovicz
Editor: Annie Sommers
Photo Researcher: Elizabeth Loving